D1709367

THAT'S GROSS!

GROSS THINGS ABOUT YOUR FOOD

By Maria Nelson

Gareth Stevens
Publishing

Please visit our website, www.garethstevens.com. For a free color catalog of all our high-quality books, call toll free 1-800-542-2595 or fax 1-877-542-2596.

Library of Congress Cataloging-in-Publication Data

Nelson, Maria.
 Gross things about your food / Maria Nelson.
     p. cm. — (That's gross!)
 Includes bibliographical references and index.
 ISBN 978-1-4339-7116-7 (pbk.)
 ISBN 978-1-4339-7117-4 (6-pack)
 ISBN 978-1-4339-7115-0 (library binding)
 1. Food adulteration and inspection—Juvenile literature. I. Title.
 TX533.N38 2013
 363.19'26—dc23

                                        2012008766

First Edition

Published in 2013 by
Gareth Stevens Publishing
111 East 14th Street, Suite 349
New York, NY 10003

Copyright © 2013 Gareth Stevens Publishing

Designer: Daniel Hosek
Editor: Therese Shea

Photo credits: Cover (tomatoes) , p. 1 (tomatoes) Alexander A. Trofimov/Shutterstock.com; cover (bacteria), p. 1 (bacteria) Raycat/iStockphoto.com; pp. 4–5 © (microorganisms) humonia/ iStockphoto.com; p. 5 (main image) NightAndDayImages/iStockphoto.com; pp. 6 (apples), 7 (pumpkin), 12, 13 (all images), 20 (haggis) iStockphoto/Thinkstock.com; p. 8 Stockbyte/ Thinkstock.com; p. 9 (main image) Fuse/Getty Images; p. 9 (label) Kathy Dewar/ iStockphoto.com; p. 11 (bread) Fotosearch/Getty Images; p. 11 (yeast) Steve Gschmeissner/ Science Photo Library/Getty Images; pp. 15 (main image), 21 Hemera/Thinkstock.com; p. 15 (*E. coli*) Ingram Publishing/Thinkstock.com; p. 17 Photo Researchers/Getty Images; p. 19 incposterco/iStockphoto.com; p. 20 (octopus) Image Source/Thinkstock.com.

Printed in the United States of America

CPSIA compliance information: Batch #CS12GS: For further information contact Gareth Stevens, New York, New York at 1-800-542-2595.

CONTENTS

Words in the glossary appear in **bold** type the first time they are used in the text.

WHAT WE DON'T KNOW

Our bodies need food to live. Food helps us grow, move, and stay healthy. But there are many things we'd probably rather not know about our food.

Some of the grossest things happen to food when it's being prepared. For example, tiny bug parts get trapped in packaged foods. **Microorganisms** are allowed to grow on beef to make it taste better. Sometimes the food itself might seem gross, especially foods eaten in other parts of the world. Want to get grossed out? Read on!

microorganisms that age beef

If you've eaten a steak at a restaurant, you've probably eaten aged beef—and the microorganisms that make it tasty.

5

THAT'S ROTTEN!

After a few days in your kitchen, a banana starts to turn brown. Though it becomes sweeter, not everyone finds the mushy brown spots tasty.

As soon as a fruit or vegetable is removed from the plant it grows on, it starts to break down, or decay. **Fungi** and **bacteria** cause the decay. Spots formed by a layer of fungus called mold may grow on the food. This causes the fruit or vegetable to "go bad." Have you ever seen a rotten potato? It's black and smells bad, too!

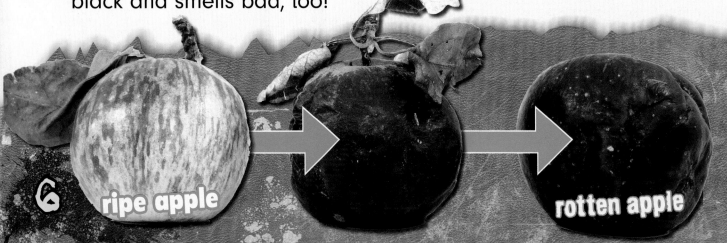

ripe apple

rotten apple

If a fruit or vegetable is kept in the wrong conditions, such as being too warm or wet, the decaying process speeds up.

9

PRESERVATIVES

Read the **ingredients** on your favorite box of cereal. You probably won't recognize some of them. Most packaged foods contain preservatives, which are things that help them last longer. Many preservatives are **chemicals** that keep foods' colors, smells, and tastes from changing. Others keep foods' ingredients from separating.

Some people are against using preservatives in foods. They may have an **allergy** to a certain preservative. Or they may just want to eat foods that are natural.

Gross or Cool?

Preservatives keep foods fresh—sometimes for years!

Value
BEANS
in tomato sauce

Preservatives are found in cocoa, crackers, and even meat.

Nutrition Facts

ts: Water, Sugar, Soy Sauce (Water, Whea
Vegetable Oil (Soybean and/or Canola), Distilled
Marmalade (Sugar, Oranges, Corn Syrup, Pectin, Ci
Sodium Benzoate as a preservative), Lime Juice, Orange Ju
oncentrate, Sesame Oil, contains 2% or less of: Salt, Garlic, G
Lemon Juice Concentrate, Spices, Onion Powder, Natural Flav
Monosodium Glutamate, Xanthan Gum, Sesame Seed, Caramel C

Amount Per Serving	%DV*	Amount Per Serving	
		Total Carb 8g	
Total Fat 4g	6%	Dietary Fiber 0g	
Sat Fat 0g	0%	Sugars 7g	
Trans Fat 0g		Protein 0g	
Cholest. 0mg	0%		
Sodium 450mg	19%		
Vitamin A 0% • Vitamin C 4% • Calci			

Size 2 Tbsp (30g)
gs 16
gs 70
40

Values (DV) are
0 calorie diet.

9

FAVORITE FERMENTED FOODS

Some kinds of bacteria and fungi can be harmful to eat. However, in order to make some of our favorite foods, we help "good" microorganisms grow! This process is called fermentation. The conditions and supplies needed for fermentation are different for each food.

Pickles, chocolate, yogurt, and even bread depend on fermentation to become the foods we know. A fungus called yeast is added to bread dough to break down the sugar in it. It gives off gas, making the dough rise.

Controlling **temperature** is one important part of the fermentation process. The right temperature keeps the good microorganisms alive.

yeast seen through a microscope

Gross or Cool?

The yeast added to bread eats a sugar called glucose and gives off a gas called carbon dioxide.

Fungi play a part in making cheese. They're added to the outside or inside of the cheese, depending on the kind of cheese being made. Then, the cheese is kept in conditions that help the fungi "ripen" it.

Have you ever eaten blue cheese on a salad? Have you spread the French cheese called Brie on a cracker? Both of these cheeses get their special taste from the fungi that grow on and in them. Maybe it sounds gross, but cheese wouldn't taste right without them!

Gross or Cool?

A sheep's milk cheese called casu marzu is made using **maggots**! It's illegal in many countries.

The blue lines and spots in blue cheese are called marbling. Marbling is mold!

13

FOOD SAFETY

E. coli is a common bacteria. Many kinds of *E. coli* are harmless, but some are deadly. *E. coli* that pollute, or contaminate, your food are most often found in raw meat, soft cheeses, and on raw fruits and vegetables. Other sources are unclean water and animals, especially cows, sheep, and goats.

The best way to keep a kitchen safe from harmful bacteria is to wash your hands before and after preparing food. Any surface that comes into contact with raw meat should also be cleaned well.

Gross or Cool?

Some good kinds of *E. coli* live inside your body and inside the bodies of animals.

In 2011, 60 people became ill after eating lettuce contaminated with a bad kind of E. coli.

E. coli seen through a microscope

15

THAT'S NOT FOOD!

Have you ever found part of a bug in your salad dressing? Unfortunately, even if you don't see it, gross stuff may still be in some foods!

Small amounts of fly parts, hair, and other nonfood things can be found in many foods. The US Food and Drug Administration (FDA) makes rules so people aren't harmed by foods. For example, up to about 25 milligrams (0.0009 ounce) of sand and "grit" can be present in about 1/2 cup (100 g) of peanut butter.

Gross or Cool?

Part of the FDA's job is telling companies how much "foreign matter," or anything that isn't food, can be in the food they produce.

Fruit flies like this one like tomato sauce a lot. The FDA allows a very small number of fruit fly eggs in tomato sauces.

TO SPRAY OR NOT TO SPRAY

Many farmers use chemical sprays called pesticides to keep their crops safe from bugs. It's also common for animals to be given **hormones** that make them grow bigger or produce more milk.

Some people don't agree with these practices. They buy **organic** foods instead. Organic fruits and vegetables are only treated with pesticides made of natural products, if at all. Organic meat and dairy products come from animals that only eat organic feed and haven't been given any hormones.

This airplane, called a crop duster, sprays a pesticide on farm crops.

19

THE "ICK" HEARD 'ROUND THE WORLD

Are you an adventurous eater? Some people around the world eat much differently than we do. Some of what they think is tasty we might find gross.

Haggis, a traditional dish from Scotland, is made of a lamb or sheep's heart, lungs, and liver mixed with oats and spices. In Japan, it's common to eat octopus—and sometimes it's still alive! However, remember that people in other places may think the foods you eat are gross, too!

octopus

haggis

Food Safety Tips

- Store foods at the proper temperature. Your refrigerator should be set at 40°F (4°C) or below. Your freezer should be kept at 0°F (−18°C) or below.

- Buy fruits and vegetables without any "bad" spots.

- Wash all produce before you eat it.

- Keep raw meat and eggs separate from other raw foods.

- Cook all meats thoroughly.

- Wash your hands and the surfaces you use before and after preparing food.

- Visit foodsafety.gov to learn how long it's safe to keep different kinds of food.

Gross or Cool?

In some countries, bugs are on the menu. People in Nigeria eat locusts. They call them "desert shrimp."

GLOSSARY

allergy: an overreaction by the body (including sneezing and watery eyes) to something that isn't usually harmful

bacteria: tiny, single-celled organisms. Many kinds are helpful. Some can cause illnesses in humans.

chemical: matter that can be mixed with other matter to cause changes

fungus: a living thing that is somewhat like a plant, but doesn't make its own food, have leaves, or have a green color. Fungi include yeast, molds, and mushrooms.

hormone: a chemical made in the body that tells another part of the body what to do

ingredient: a food that is mixed with other foods

locust: a grasshopper found in warm places that lives in large populations and eats crops

maggot: a wormlike young fly

microorganism: a very small living thing that can only be seen under a microscope

organic: occurring or growing naturally

temperature: how hot or cold something is

FOR MORE INFORMATION

Books

King, Bart. *The Big Book of Gross Stuff*. Layton, UT: Gibbs Smith, 2010.

Perritano, John. *The Most Disgusting Foods on the Planet*. Mankato, MN: Capstone Press, 2012.

Rosenberg, Pam. *Eek! Icky, Sticky, Gross Stuff in Your Food*. Mankato, MN: The Child's World, 2008.

Websites

Kids World: Food Safety
www.ncagr.gov/cyber/kidswrld/foodsafe/
Learn about different kinds of bacteria and how to keep your food safe from them.

Making Blue Cheese
biology.clc.uc.edu/fankhauser/cheese/blue_cheese/blue_cheese.htm
Read about how to make this tasty—and moldy!—cheese at home.

INDEX